How To Write A Resume

Resume Templates

By Obinna Kaluorji

COPYRIGHT PAGE

All rights reserved. No part of this book may be republished in any form or by any means, including photocopying, scanning or otherwise without prior written permission to the copyright holder.

Copyright © 2023 Obinna Kaluorji

Table of Contents

DEDICATION 4

INTRODUCTION 5

WHAT IS A RESUME 6

WHY PACKAGE YOUR RESUME 7

BEST PRACTICES IN CREATING A RESUME 9

RESUME TEMPLATES 11

   Template 1 12

   Template 2 19

   Template 3 26

   Template 4 (Experienced) 32

RESUME REFERENCES TEMPLATE 37

OTHER BOOKS BY THE AUTHOR 38

DEDICATION

I would like to dedicate this book to the following persons for the role they played to the existence of this book;

My wife; for all her encouragements and support. For believing in me and helping me to be a better version of myself. For making me know how unique I am and letting me know that all I do is always the best.

My mum; who single handedly trained us (5 boys) and saw us through school after our dad left us at an early age

My siblings; for all their love and encouragements and for their support at on point or the other.

My relatives; for the role they play in my life and for all their encouragements.

INTRODUCTION

A resume is a document that summarizes everything about you.

Your resume is like you in the hands of your prospective employer. With a perfect resume, your prospective employer can decide to skip interview questions because he already saw all he need in an employer in your resume.

Since your prospective employer will have lots of resume that are similar to yours in his/her hand to read through in a limited time, there is need you captured the heart of your prospective employer in that limited time right from the beginning of your resume.

If your resume is not well packaged, your prospective employer might trash your resume even before going through the whole resume.

You are free to use any of the resume templates in this book to form your own resume.

What is a Resume

A resume is a document that summarizes everything about you.

A resume is the first document to tender to your prospective employer that highlights your qualifications, schools attended, former employments, certifications obtained, your strengths, your weakness, hobbies, your home address, your state of origin etc.

With just your resume, your prospective employer can have up to 90% of the details he needs to know about you.

Your resume is the best document you can use to sell yourself and convince your prospective employer without having to see your prospective employer in person.

Since you already know that your resume is the best way to sell yourself to your prospective employer, there is need that you package your resume, make it very detailed, error free and very attractive.

Why package your resume

Your resume is like you in the hands of your prospective employer. With a perfect resume, your prospective employer can decide to skip interview questions because he already saw all he need in an employer in your resume.

Since you already know that your resume is like you in the hands of your prospective employer, there is need you package resume. The impression you will create in the heart of your prospective employer through your resume might be a lasting one if your resume is detailed and on point.

You prospective employer will probably have lots of resume that are similar to yours and if you can not captured the heart of your prospective employer from the beginning of your resume, he/she might trash your resume even before going through the whole resume.

Three fields in your resume that attracts your prospective employer the most are;

- Your past experiences

- Your organization goals

- Your strengths and weakness
- Your certifications and lastly
- Your qualifications.

From the list above, you will notice that your qualification appeared last in the list. That simply means that your qualification is important in landing you a job but it does not matter the most. I know of someone that got a well-paying job without a qualification, that simply means that I am speaking from experience.

The most important two information your prospective employer looks for is your past experiences and your professional certifications.

That having said, if you are a fresh graduate looking for a job, focus more on getting trainings and certifications. If you are lucky to get a job, focus more on learning on the job and gathering some experience on the job. As a fresh graduate, remove your mind from the pay and gain the experience first. The experience will give you a better pay in the future.

Best Practices in creating a Resume

With your resume, you sell yourself to your prospective employer but don't over-sell yourself.

While writing your resume, there are some rules you need to follow that will help you get that job faster. The rules are highlighted below;

- Always start your resume with your organization goal. Your organization goal is "what value you intend to add to your prospective organization"

- Always start your past experiences with the most recent.

- Write your references in a separate document and let your prospective employer know that you will make it available on request.

- Notify anyone you intend to use as your referee ahead of time.

- Always start your certification and qualifications with the most recent.

- Don't include what you cannot do in your resume. That can implicate you later if you finally get the job.

- Don't sound desperate in your resume. Never use words like please, help me, I beg you, consider me etc.

- Before you start writing your resume, ensure that you already all the information you need in the resume on standby. Best you write them down somewhere first before transferring them to your resume.

- Ensure that you use the right font and the best font size. Don't let the font size be too small or too big. Size 12 is always the best.

- Ensure that there is consistency in your font and your font size. Don't use a different font/font size here and a different font/font size there.

Resume templates

Before I list some resume templates you can use, want to remind you of some things to bear in mind; Always ensure that your resume is detailed enough to convey the information you have in mind and that you always start with most recent because you might not get the second chance to make that first impression.

When you are invited for an interview, look your best and always ensure that you can remember all that is in your resume even without looking at it.

The resume listed below are to guide you in creating your own resume. You are free to use any of the resume templates but ensure that you tailor it down to your information.

Below are some proven resume templates you can use to form your own resume. Some of the resume templates might have spaces where you can append your passport photograph but having a passport photograph in your resume is not a most. The focus is more on you past experiences and not on your photograph.

Template 1

LASTNAME, FIRSTNAME

7 TEST STREET LGA, TEST STATE

Email: youremail@omail.com, phone: 081111111

CAREER OBJECTIVE: Will ensure that organizational goals and objectives are achieved by doing my best and working in harmony with the existing staff.

WORK EXPERIENCE

Java Alpha Dyn Group of companies, LGA, Test state. Nigeria.

Role: Java Developer   2023

Educational Instructor, Test Academy, LGA, Test state. Nigeria

Role: Physics Instructor   2021

PERSONAL INFORMATION

Date of Birth: 8th April, 1990

Marital Status: Single

Sex: Male

State of Origin: Test State

Nationality: Nigerian

Languages: English and Igbo

Religion: Christian

TRAININGS ATTENDED

* Project management and customer relationship.

April, 2022

Self-made group of companies

* Effective Customer Relationship and Service Quality Management.

December, 2021

Institute of management and Customer Relationship group of companies.

* Preparation for life and the workplace: Skills and Strategies.

June, 2013

Skills development group of companies.

EDUCATIONAL QUALIFICATION

* Professional Postgraduate Diploma.

   December, 2022.

   Institute of management and Customer Relationship group of companies.

* Health, Safety and Environment (HSE).

   October, 2021.

   Institute of management and Customer Relationship group of companies.

* Bachelor of sciences (Technology).

   November, 2019.

   Second Class Hons, Test state university, LGA, Test State.

* Senior School Certificate Examination

    June 2012.

    Community secondary school, LGA, Test State.

* Primary School Leaving Certificate.

    2003

    All Saint's Primary School, LGA, Test state.

KEY COMPETIENCES

* Conflict Resolution: I strive to initiate peace agreement in Situations of conflict, convincing difficult Clients, scheduling events, making and Settling Issues.

* Leadership Skills: I confidently lead team, organize meetings, supervise team members and motivate Colleagues.

* Effective Communication Skills.

* Good Interpersonal Skill.

* Accountability
* Commitment to Excellence and Teamwork.

RELATED VOLUNTEER EXPERIENCES

* CDS Corp Liasson officer: Community development service.
* CDS Project Secretary: Community development service.
* Course Representative: Physics Department, Test state, University, LGA, Nigeria.

PROFESSIONAL MEMBERSHIP

*Associate Member: Institute of customer relationship group of companies.

*Graduate Member: Project Management Professionals group of companies.

AWARD

Certificate of Exemplary Performance and effective project Management, Test State, Nigeria

CORE VALUES

* Honesty, Humility, Diligence and Hard work.

LEISURE INTERESTS

Reading, playing Volleyball and engaging in analytical discussions.

REFERENCES

Available on Request.

Template 2

Passport Photo	**CAREER OBJECTIVE**: Will ensure that organizational goals and objectives are achieved by doing my best and working in harmony with the existing staff.
LASTNAME, FIRSTNAME	
ADDRESS: 7 TEST STREET LGA, TEST STATE	**WORK EXPERIENCE**
	Java Alpha Dyn Group of companies, LGA, Test state. Nigeria.
Email: youremail@omail.com	Role: Java Developer 2023
phone: 081111111	Educational Instructor, Test Academy, LGA, Test state. Nigeria
	Role: Physics Instructor 2021

PERSONAL INFORMATION

Date of Birth: 8th April, 1990

Marital Status: Single

Sex: Male

State of Origin: Test State

Nationality: Nigerian

Languages: English and Igbo

Religion: Christian

TRAININGS ATTENDED

* Project management and customer relationship.

April, 2022

Self-made group of companies

* Effective Customer Relationship and Service Quality Management.

December, 2021

Institute of management and Customer Relationship group of companies.

* Preparation for life and the workplace: Skills and Strategies.

June, 2013

Skills development group of companies.

EDUCATIONAL QUALIFICATION

* Professional Postgraduate Diploma.

December, 2022.

Institute of management and Customer Relationship group of companies.

* Health, Safety and Environment (HSE).

October, 2021.

Institute of management and Customer Relationship group of companies.

* Bachelor of sciences (Technology).

November, 2019.

Second Class Hons, Test state university, LGA, Test State.

* Senior School Certificate Examination

June 2012.

Community secondary school, LGA, Test State.

* Primary School Leaving Certificate.

2003

All Saint's Primary School, LGA, Test state.

KEY COMPETIENCES

* Conflict Resolution: I strive to initiate peace agreement in Situations of conflict, convincing difficult Clients, scheduling events, making and Settling Issues.

* Leadership Skills: I confidently lead team, organize meetings, supervise team members and motivate Colleagues.

* Effective Communication Skills.

* Good Interpersonal Skill.

* Accountability

* Commitment to Excellence and Teamwork.

RELATED VOLUNTEER EXPERIENCES

* CDS Corp Liasson officer: Community development service.

* CDS Project Secretary: Community development service.

* Course Representative: Physics Department, Test state, University, LGA, Nigeria.

PROFESSIONAL MEMBERSHIP

*Associate Member: Institute of customer relationship group of companies.

*Graduate Member: Project Management Professionals group of companies.

AWARD

Certificate of Exemplary Performance and effective project Management, Test State, Nigeria

CORE VALUES

* Honesty, Humility, Diligence and Hard work.

LEISURE INTERESTS

Reading, playing Volleyball and engaging in analytical discussions.

REFERENCES

Available on Request.

Template 3

Lastname, First name
7 TEST STREET LGA, TEST STATE
Email: youremail@omail.com, phone: 081111111

CAREER OBJECTIVE: Will ensure that organizational goals and objectives are achieved by doing my best and working in harmony with the existing staff.

WORK EXPERIENCE

Java Alpha Dyn Group of companies, LGA, Test state. Nigeria.

Role: Java Developer   2023

Educational Instructor, Test Academy, LGA, Test state. Nigeria

Role: Physics Instructor   2021

PERSONAL INFORMATION

Date of Birth: 8th April, 1990

Marital Status: Single

Sex: Male

State of Origin: Test State

Nationality: Nigerian

Languages: English and Igbo

Religion: Christian

TRAININGS ATTENDED

* Project management and customer relationship.

April, 2022

Self-made group of companies

* Effective Customer Relationship and Service Quality Management.

December, 2021

Institute of management and Customer Relationship group of companies.

* Preparation for life and the workplace: Skills and Strategies.

June, 2013

Skills development group of companies.

EDUCATIONAL QUALIFICATION

* Professional Postgraduate Diploma.

December, 2022.

Institute of management and Customer Relationship group of companies.

* Health, Safety and Environment (HSE).

October, 2021.

Institute of management and Customer Relationship group of companies.

* Bachelor of sciences (Technology).

    November, 2019.

    Second Class Hons, Test state university, LGA, Test State.

* Senior School Certificate Examination

    June 2012.

    Community secondary school, LGA, Test State.

* Primary School Leaving Certificate.

    2003

    All Saint's Primary School, LGA, Test state.

KEY COMPETIENCES

* Conflict Resolution: I strive to initiate peace agreement in Situations of conflict, convincing difficult Clients, scheduling events, making and Settling Issues.

* Leadership Skills: I confidently lead team, organize meetings, supervise team members and motivate Colleagues.

* Effective Communication Skills.

* Good Interpersonal Skill.

* Accountability

* Commitment to Excellence and Teamwork.

RELATED VOLUNTEER EXPERIENCES

* CDS Corp Liasson officer: Community development service.

* CDS Project Secretary: Community development service.

* Course Representative: Physics Department, Test state, University, LGA, Nigeria.

PROFESSIONAL MEMBERSHIP

*Associate Member: Institute of customer relationship group of companies.

*Graduate Member: Project Management Professionals group of companies.

AWARD

Certificate of Exemplary Performance and effective project Management, Test State, Nigeria

CORE VALUES

* Honesty, Humility, Diligence and Hard work.

LEISURE INTERESTS

Reading, playing Volleyball and engaging in analytical discussions.

REFERENCES

Available on Request.

Template 4 (Experienced)

LASTNAME, FIRSTNAME
7 TEST STREET LGA, TEST STATE

Yourname@omail.com

081111111

OBJECTIVE

Will ensure that organizational goals and objectives are achieved by doing my best and working in harmony with the existing staff.

Profile	I am an Electrical Engineer at Company Plc. My area of core competence is in coding, repairs and general support. In the course of my career in Company Plc, have developed and gathered deep professional Techno-Functional experience

	with Electrical Troubleshooting, implementation, end user support, coding, repairs, testing, training, information & systems control in the technology industry.
Background	**Functional Expertise** - **Software Testing Skills**: User Acceptance (UAT) Testing, System Integration (SIT) Testing, Regression, Penetration and Unit Testing - repairs/support skills - Problem solving and analytical skills. - Troubleshooting and root cause analysis skills. - Quick learning ability. - Excellent team player - Great interpersonal relation and communication skills. - Ability to adapt to changing work demands and conditions. - **Project Delivery:** Plan, Execute, Monitor & Control project execution and Close projects

	Past Trainings/Workshops Attended - Troubleshooting and Foundation Training **Education and Certifications** - Bachelor Degree (BSC), Inter-spark University. - Expert IQ Acquisition. - Executive Master in Project Management

Selected Relevant Experience

Troubleshooting Delivery.	2023 - till date
Position held	**Troubleshooting Consultant**

Key Responsibilities:

- Troubleshooting and Coding
- Acts as single point of contact between the Application support team and the customer.
- Provide 2nd level support in resolving all

customer application related incidents
- Analyze issues/incidents and ensure they are closed within Service Level Agreement
- Provide both remote and onsite support on customer application software.
- Escalation of problems where necessary and monitor the progress of problem resolutions.
- Establishes detection and preventive actions and application modifications to avoid recurring problems.
- Active participation on live meeting/conference calls amongst clients.
- Identifying application known errors and problem trends and for finding permanent solutions.

- Deployment of new / modified custom source codes on customer portal.
- Attend troubleshooting sessions with customers and our IT team for new development and deployments.
- Supporting for resolutions of application end of life related issues.
- Keeping tracks of Change Request and updates from customers.
- All other tasks assigned by senior managers

Project Experience	
Project	**QUI Testing (2021 - 2023)**
Position held	**Troubleshooting analyst**

Primary Responsibilities:
- Customer QUI System solution testing
- QUI System solution troubleshooting
- QUI application and functionality testing
- Activation of the QUI solution
- QUI user experience testing
- Repairs and troubleshooting of encountered errors on the QUI application

BIO DATA:

Sex: Male.

Marital status: Married

Date of Birth: 11/10/1990

State of origin: Test state

Nationality: Nigeria.

REFEREEES

Available on request.

RESUME REFERENCES TEMPLATE

LASTNAME, FIRSTNAME

7 TEST STREET LGA, TEST STATE

Email: youremail@omail.com, phone: 081111111

REFERENCES:

Rev. Test Bessy
Ascendum group of companies, LGA,
Test State.
Email: test2@mail.com
Tel: 08022222

Mr. Brainy Boost
Teste Government House, LGA
Test State.
Tel: 08033333

Mrs. Elom Bally
Dudem Girls Secondary School, LGA,
Test State.
Tel: 07044444

Other Books by The Author

 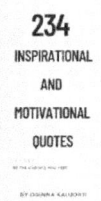 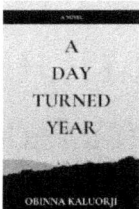 

www.ingramcontent.com/pod-product-compliance
Lightning Source LLC
Chambersburg PA
CBHW050322220526
45465CB00005B/2089